The "Would You Rather?" Game for Couples, Dates, & Parties: Sexy and Naughty Conversation Starters to Explore Fantasies and Kinks, Spice Things Up, and Push Boundaries (All While Laughing)

By Amber Cole

So... let's play a game. Ready?

Would you rather...?

Have you heard of this game before? You may not have engaged in it since you were a teenager or even earlier, but it's time to bring it back with a hot and sexy spin. This is "Would you rather..." the adult version, and it's designed to help you learn about your partner (or partners) and open up your mind.

How does that happen? Well, you might never know what you like unless it's placed right in front of you. And furthermore, you might never know what your partner likes unless they are forced to tell you directly. This fun little conversation game nails two birds with one stone. It gets you out of your comfort zone and presents possibilities that you may never have considered, and it allows you to see your partner in a new, open, and nonjudgmental light. Scenarios will be presented, and seeds will be planted for future growth. You might think you're about to embark on a night of ordinary lovemaking (hey, nothing wrong with that unless vanilla becomes a negative term for you), and suddenly, you notice a whip or a bowl of ice cream on the bedside table.

Well, where did that idea come from?

But most of all, this is just a fun game to get to know people better. It forces you to go beyond your comfort zone, when that might not be your first instinct, or you might even feel shy about it. So read on with an open mind and sense of anticipation for what you are about to learn about yourself and your partner.

Each page has a "would you rather...?" question. No skipping, no exceptions. You must answer it, and so must your partner. If you find that you are taking too long to get through questions, feel free to institute a sixty-second thinking time limit! Don't think too deeply, just say what's on your mind—after all, that's the point of the conversation game.

Here's another tip to facilitate this game for maximum fun: if you answer a question, your partner has to ask you at least three follow-up questions to dig deeply into the answer and truly understand you better. No dodging questions allowed. And of course, you must do the same whenever they answer a question.

ONE

Would you rather have sex with all the lights on OR all the lights off?

TWO

Would you rather orgasm from oral sex OR give an orgasm through oral sex?

THREE

Would you rather have early-morning sex OR have late-night sex?

FOUR

Would you rather get caught having sex in public OR find out you were being watched after the fact?

FIVE

Would you rather have sex with someone who is noisy throughout sex OR someone who only screams during an orgasm?

SIX

Would you rather have ice cream eaten off your body OR eat it off your partner's body?

SEVEN

Would you rather have perpetual, never-ending orgasms daily OR only one orgasm per month?

EIGHT

Would you rather have sex in a Jacuzzi/bathtub OR the kitchen?

NINE

Would you rather have sex with someone who is super sexy but unskilled OR have sex with someone who is super skilled in bed but not attractive?

TEN

Would you rather have 20 minutes of foreplay and 2 minutes of sex OR 2 minutes of foreplay and 20 minutes of sex?

ELEVEN

Would you rather have a series of "meh" orgasms OR one really amazing orgasm?

TWELVE

Would you rather be terrible at foreplay OR be terrible at sex?

THIRTEEN

Would you rather have sex with Beyoncé OR Shakira?

FOURTEEN

Would you rather have sex with Brad Pitt OR Johnny Depp?

FIFTEEN

Would you rather be dominant OR be submissive in bed (put another way, take control or have your partner take control in bed)?

SIXTEEN

Would you rather sleep with a virgin OR sleep with someone of the same sex?

SEVENTEEN

Would you rather be a sugar mama/daddy OR have a sugar mama/daddy?

EIGHTEEN

Would you rather sleep with a superior for a promotion OR have a subordinate sleep with you for a promotion?

NINETEEN

Would you rather have rough sex most of the time OR tender sex most of the time?

TWENTY

Would you rather have sex standing OR have sex sitting?

TWENTY-ONE

Would you rather have your anus played with OR play with someone else's anus?

TWENTY-TWO

Would you rather have sex with two people of the opposite sex OR two people of the same sex?

TWENTY-THREE

Would you rather have sex with someone who is deaf OR someone who is blind?

TWENTY-FOUR

Would you rather be blindfolded during sex OR handcuffed?

TWENTY-FIVE

Would you rather sleep with your ex OR masturbate at home?

TWENTY-SIX

Would you rather be tied up and whipped OR do the tying and whipping?

TWENTY-SEVEN

Would you rather have sex 14 times a week OR have sex 2 times a week?

TWENTY-EIGHT

Would you rather eat your partner's ass OR have them eat yours?

TWENTY-NINE

Would you rather your partner always have bad breath OR your partner have really dirty nails?

THIRTY

Would you rather walk outside your block naked OR have your partner look at your porn search history?

THIRTY-ONE

Would you rather have sex with someone who takes 5 seconds to orgasm OR someone who takes 3 hours to orgasm?

THIRTY-TWO

Would you rather have sex only in doggy style OR never have sex in doggy style?

THIRTY-THREE

Would you rather have sex in a public restroom OR in the back of a car?

THIRTY-FOUR

Would you rather have sex when drunk OR have sex when on other drugs?

THIRTY-FIVE

Would you rather have sex with someone who has never trimmed their pubic hair OR have sex with someone who hasn't showered for 3 days?

THIRTY-SIX

Would you rather be brought to orgasm orally OR brought to orgasm by hand(s)?

THIRTY-SEVEN

Would you rather never please your partner sexually OR never be pleased by your partner sexually?

THIRTY-EIGHT

Would you rather be bitten so hard there are bruises OR be spanked so hard there are bruises?

THIRTY-NINE

Would you rather touch yourself in private OR touch yourself in front of your partner?

FORTY

Would you rather be in the same room watching people have sex OR have people in the room watching you have sex?

FORTY-ONE

Would you rather have sex with someone 10 years older than you OR have sex with someone 10 years younger than you?

FORTY-TWO

Would you rather have porn-like dirty talk and moaning during sex OR have complete and utter silence during sex?

FORTY-THREE

Would you rather have sex with someone who wants to suck your toes OR have sex with someone who likes their toes to be sucked?

FORTY-FOUR

Would you rather be choked during sex OR be slapped in the face during sex?

FORTY-FIVE

Would you rather be greeted at the door by your partner in leather and nipple clamps OR be greeted at the door with a glass of wine and soft jazz playing in the background?

FORTY-SIX

Would you rather cuddle after sex OR immediately wash off after sex?

FORTY-SEVEN

Would you rather have your partner use a sex toy on you, OR use a sex toy on your partner?

FORTY-EIGHT

Would you rather have sex in public OR masturbate in public?

FORTY-NINE

Would you rather give a golden shower OR receive a golden shower?

FIFTY

Would you rather lose control during sex OR make your partner lose control during sex?

FIFTY-ONE

Would you rather have anal sex OR have period sex?

FIFTY-TWO

Would you rather watch porn together OR read an erotic novel together?

FIFTY-THREE

Would you rather be woken up by oral sex OR be woken up by sex (penetration)?

FIFTY-FOUR

Would you rather only be on top during sex OR only be on the bottom during sex?

FIFTY-FIVE

Would you rather roleplay professor and student OR roleplay doctor and patient?

FIFTY-SIX

Would you rather roleplay as flirting strangers in public OR roleplay as prostitute and client in public?

FIFTY-SEVEN

Would you rather watch a porn scene and copy them position by position and sound by sound OR simply have it play in the background for inspiration?

FIFTY-EIGHT

Would you rather talk dirty in public OR receive dirty texts and photos in public?

FIFTY-NINE

Would you rather have anal sex OR penetrate your partner anally?

SIXTY

Would you rather use ropes during sex OR be forced to obey your partner during sex?

SIXTY-ONE

Would you rather have a happy-ending massage (manual only) OR receive oral sex?

SIXTY-TWO

Would you rather have shower sex OR have beach sex?

SIXTY-THREE

Would you rather have a threesome with your partner and a friend OR have a threesome with your partner and a stranger?

SIXTY-FOUR

Would you rather have hot wax dripped onto you OR have ice cubes used on you?

SIXTY-FIVE

Would you rather please a partner 10 times a day OR be pleased by a partner 10 times a day?

SIXTY-SIX

Would you rather have sex without using your mouth OR have sex without using your hands?

SIXTY-SEVEN

Would you rather have mediocre sex with multiple partners OR great sex with one partner?

SIXTY-EIGHT

Would you rather make a sex video and watch it with your partner OR make an audio recording only and listen to it with your partner?

SIXTY-NINE

Would you rather swallow semen OR toss a salad?

SEVENTY

Would you rather motorboat large breasts OR motorboat a large ass?

SEVENTY-ONE

Would you rather have sex on the first date OR hold hands on the first date?

SEVENTY-TWO

Would you rather sleep together without having sex OR have sex and leave after?

SEVENTY-THREE

Would you rather have sex in black lingerie OR have sex in a naughty schoolgirl outfit?

SEVENTY-FOUR

Would you rather make uninterrupted eye contact during sex OR no communication at all during sex?

SEVENTY-FIVE

Would you rather swap partners with a couple (your most attractive friends) OR pick up strangers at a bar?

SEVENTY-SIX

Would you rather visit to a nudist colony OR go to a swingers party?

SEVENTY-SEVEN

Would you rather have sex in a church OR have sex within earshot of your grandparents?

SEVENTY-EIGHT

Would you rather go to a strip club OR go to a brothel?

SEVENTY-NINE

Would you rather have an erection/be wet for 22 hours a day OR have an erection/be wet for 2 hours a day?

EIGHTY

Would you rather marry a virgin OR marry someone who has had 100 partners?

EIGHTY-ONE

Would you rather have sex at 6 thrusts a minute (to completion) OR have sex at 40 thrusts a minute (to completion)?

EIGHTY-TWO

Would you rather watch a sex tape of your friends OR watch them have sex on a faraway balcony?

EIGHTY-THREE

Would you rather have sex with someone with no limbs OR have sex with someone who is deaf and blind?

EIGHTY-FOUR

Would you rather be shaved by your partner OR be sensually massaged by your partner?

EIGHTY-FIVE

Would you rather have "outercourse" by titfucking OR have "outercourse" by having sex with someone's buttocks (not anal penetration)?

EIGHTY-SIX

Would you rather use a sex swing during sex OR have sex in a room of mirrors?

EIGHTY-SEVEN

Would you rather involve a butt plug in sex OR a cock ring in sex?

EIGHTY-EIGHT

Would you rather attend an orgy OR post sex pictures on the Internet?

EIGHTY-NINE

Would you rather have period sex OR accidentally get sperm in your eye?

NINETY

Would you rather have sex in a naughty nurse outfit OR have sex in a nun outfit?

NINETY-ONE

Would you rather receive a facial OR pass out during an orgasm?

NINETY-TWO

Would you rather douse yourself in massage oil during sex OR have sex in the shower?

NINETY-THREE

Would you rather be choked during sex OR be anally fingered during sex?

NINETY-FOUR

Would you rather skinny dip at a popular beach OR get caught masturbating by your partner?

NINETY-FIVE

Would you rather drink sperm OR toss a salad?

NINETY-SIX

Would you rather be the more attractive part of a couple OR the uglier part of a couple?

NINETY-SEVEN

Would you rather sext all day OR have a quickie during lunch?

NINETY-EIGHT

Would you rather have sex with someone who is 4 feet tall OR have sex with someone who is 7 feet tall?

NINETY-NINE

Would you rather have sex with someone who fakes orgasms but is amazing in bed OR have sex with someone who is mediocre in bed but has only honest orgasms?

ONE HUNDRED

Would you rather have an "accident" during anal OR scream someone else's name when you orgasm?

ONE HUNDRED AND ONE

Would you rather have whipped cream eaten off your genitals OR be spanked with a leather riding crop?

ONE HUNDRED AND TWO

Would you rather have rough sex that caused injuries OR boring sex that makes you yawn?

ONE HUNDRED AND THREE

Would you rather watch lesbian porn OR watch gay porn?

ONE HUNDRED AND FOUR

Would you rather have 9/10 orgasms every week OR one 10/10 orgasm a month?

ONE HUNDRED AND FIVE

Would you rather have only oral sex for the rest of your life OR live without it completely?

ONE HUNDRED AND SIX

Would you rather give someone oral sex who tastes bad OR give someone oral sex who smells bad?

ONE HUNDRED AND SEVEN

Would you rather make an ugly face when you orgasm OR make donkey noises when you orgasm?

ONE HUNDRED AND EIGHT

Would you rather discover that your last sex partner was a cousin OR locked up in jail for murder?

www.ingramcontent.com/pod-product-compliance
Lightning Source LLC
Chambersburg PA
CBHW071359080526
44587CB00017B/3130